Feed Your Family of Four for

$4

a Day

By Mack and Celia Webb

Pilinut Press, Inc.

Meet the Authors

Celia learned the art of cooking as a grade-schooler from her mother, who also taught her how to feed a large family on a small budget. Celia's cooking and budgeting know-how proved invaluable when years later she left home to earn a degree in Business from Indiana University, Bloomington, Indiana and a degree in Systems Engineering from the Naval Postgraduate School, Monterey, California. Celia continues to refine her culinary skills, experimenting with recipes and ingredients to create delicious, budget-friendly meals.

Mack likes to cook, but likes growing and raising food even more. He embraces the challenges that come with his mission of providing plenty of healthful food for his family as inexpensively as possible. Mack's degree in Horticulture from the University of Maryland has served him well in his organic-gardening endeavors. The knowledge he gained has helped him and Celia raise much of what appears on their dining table. Eggs are included courtesy of their four delightful hens.

Together Mack and Celia constantly seek out ways to improve quality of life and find pleasure in providing you with enjoyable, informative, first-rate books and articles published by Pilinut Press.

Learn More About Pilinut Press

Pilinut Press, Inc. is an independent publishing company founded in 2006. Our quality books are available through on-line book vendors like Amazon.com and your local bookstore as a special order item. In addition to our books, we support our readers and educators through our **Reference Desk** feature on the company website which offers free articles, lesson plans, bookmarks, interviews, printable teaching aids, and more. Check us out at

www.pilinutpress.com.

Feed Your Family of Four for

$4

a Day

The pilinut is the edible seed of the *Canarium ovatum* tree which is native to Southeast Asia. Tasting like sweet almonds, it is eaten for its health benefits including prevention of anemia and for nourishment of the brain and nervous system.

Library of Congress Control Number: 2011945964
Printed in Warrenton, Virginia
ISBN-10: 0-9779576-8-3
ISBN-13: 978-0-9779576-8-2

Book and cover design by Celia Webb
Cover Art by Celia Webb

Pilinut Press, Inc.
www.pilinutpress.com

Table of Contents

Introduction

Food. Without a doubt any who would survive must have it. It is a basic need, but acquiring nutrient-rich food in its proper amount and variety can be anything but basic. Most people have to pay for their food, and wildly fluctuating food costs can leave stomachs grumbling for the want of sustenance. Fear not; you can serve up delicious, nutritious, balanced meals five times a day to your family of four. In lean times, you can even keep your family going on $4 a day. This book shows you how so let's get to it.

Planning meal sizes

Age and gender will dictate the calories needed for a given person. Use the chart below to plan meal sizes for each member of your family. Determining the calories in your food items will allow you to make adjustments to your family members' energy needs. Read labels and produce cards to learn what each food provides. (See appendix D for an example of a food label.)

Each day's menu in the 30 day meal plan contains about 1500 calories per person. Make adjustments to the meal size for each person as needed.

Time	Carbohydrate	Vegetable	Fruit	Meat or Bean	Milk
Breakfast	2		1	1 or at snack	1
Snack	1		1	1 or at breakfast	
Lunch	1	2		1	2
Snack			1		1
Dinner	2	2	1	2	
Snack			1	1	

What is a serving size?

Read package labels to avoid overestimating a portion size and then measure out the food. A food scale is handy for this purpose. You will then be serving correct portion sizes for optimal health while stretching your food dollar. Here are some general guidelines.

Carbohydrate	Vegetable	Fruit	Meat or Bean	Milk
½ cup cooked noodles	½ cup cooked vegetable	One small fruit (apple, orange, etc.)	2 eggs	8 oz. milk
½ cup cooked potatoes	1 cup raw vegetable	½ cup fresh fruit	3 oz. any meat	8 oz. yogurt
½ cup cooked rice		¼ cup dried fruit	½ cup cooked beans	1 oz. cheese
5 or 6 crackers		½ cup canned fruit	¼ cup nuts	
1 slice bread				
½ cup couscous				

Even as we write this book, food prices are on the move. Some prices are creeping up and some are sliding down. One thing is certain; the prices you pay for food this week will not be the same as the prices you paid last week, at least not for all items. So to help feed your family from week to week and stay on or near your dollar budget, do not adhere rigidly to buying the same name brand food items every time you shop and learn to make creative substitutions when planning your meals. As an example, a pound of lentils typically sells for less than a pound of beans and can be a substitute in most recipes calling for beans.

The food items listed in this book are foods that will always give you the most value and nutrition for your money, no matter what the economy does. The recipes and menus here squeeze every cent you spend to give your family the deepest flavors and the highest nutrition your budget allows.

Menu Planning

- The following menu plan provides nutritious meals at minimal cost. These meals are designed to provide sufficient variety to include all the necessary proteins, carbohydrates, oils and fats, vitamins, and minerals humans require for good general health. Feel free to move meals around according to the supplies you have available.

- Creative substitution is an excellent skill to have. If the recipe calls for one thing that you do not have on hand, it is helpful to know if other items can be substituted. Some substitutions may change the flavor somewhat but you still end up with a tasty repast. For instance you can substitute ground turkey for ground beef or pork and generally save money since it is usually cheaper. Often one vegetable can be substituted for another particularly in soups, stews, and casseroles. If the recipe suggests serving an entrée with potatoes, you can try it with rice, couscous, noodles, or over bread or toast.

- Limit sweets, chips, and sugared drinks. These items do not offer much in the way of nutritional value, they tend to be high in empty calories which lead to weight gain, and they cost a lot for what they provide. Limiting them to special occasions makes sense both health- and budget-wise.

Cooking and general tips for best nutrition

- Rise up and drink 16 ounces of water. Consume the water over a period of at least 10 minutes. Your body needs H_2O in order to properly digest the meals you eat. If you are dehydrated, even slightly, food digestion will be less efficient and your body will not absorb as many nutrients from the meals you eat. So start your water consumption early in your day.

- Measure your food to avoid over eating and stretch food dollars. Americans in general do not have a good mental picture of the actual serving size of different types of food. A serving of meat for example is 3 ounces, about the size of a deck of cards. Therefore, if you order the 12-ounce steak at the local steak emporium, you can make four 3 ounces servings from that steak.

- Since you will take great care to choose the choicest, most nutritious food your budget will allow, make sure you extract as much of those nutrients as possible by chewing each bite to a cream before sending it to your stomach.

- Eat at least one soup meal everyday. Homemade soups can be very nutritious, filling, and a good use of your food dollar. It is a great way to use leftover vegetables and meats. Make a big pot of soup and eat it down the week. If you make more soup than you can finish within 5 days, freeze half for later use. Here is a simple soup recipe. Feel free to substitute whatever you have.

Hearty Soup
1 lb ground turkey (frozen is fine)
1 small onion
½ can of tomato sauce (about 7 oz.), or tomato soup, or fresh chopped or pureed tomatoes (freeze any extra for use in next week's soup)
½ cup dry noodles any type
1 cup potatoes or sweet potatoes, ½-inch cubes
3 cups chopped vegetables any type, in any combination for a total of 3 cups (green beans, corn, carrots, peppers, greens, etc.)
2 bouillon cubes or 2 teaspoons salt
1 teaspoon oregano
1 teaspoon basil
Water

In a large pot, brown the ground turkey. Add onions and cook until translucent. Add ½ cup water and dislodge the flavorful browning on the bottom of the pan. Add all other ingredients. Add enough water to bring the contents of the pot to within 1 inch of the lip of the pot. Bring to a boil. Lower heat and simmer for 30 minutes. Stir once or twice to make sure the noodles and potatoes do not stick to the bottom. Serving size = 1 cup.

- Casseroles, chilis, and stews are also cost effective ways of eating.
- Proteins are normally the most expensive part of your food budget. The least expensive sources of protein are eggs, ground meats (particularly in the frozen food section), milk, beans, and peanut butter. Plan your menus around these sources. (Dry beans which you cook yourself are more cost-effective than canned beans.)
- Be creative with whatever foods you get from free sources. If you get more than you can use before it will spoil, cook it and freeze it for later use.
- Eat 4 to 6 meals a day. Breakfast, light snack, lunch, light snack, and dinner. You might wish to add a light snack about 1 hour before bedtime. Eating this way ensures your blood sugar does not drop drastically and you do not get extra hungry and eat too much at any one sitting.

- Budget and calorie smart snacks are included under the menu section. Pay careful attention to the serving sizes of these snacks to stay on track.
- Water is vital for proper bodily functions. The general recommendation for water consumption is to drink eight (8 oz.) glasses of water every day for a total of 64 ounces. If you engage in sports or live in a hot climate, drink half your body weight in ounces (i.e. if you weigh 150 pounds, then drink 75 ounces a day).
- Eat oatmeal for breakfast at least two or three times a week. It is inexpensive, filling, and nutritionally good for you.
- Noodles are the basis of many cost-effective meals. Think spaghetti, macaroni and cheese, lasagna, baked ziti, and so on.
- Baking your own bread is cheaper than buying it in a store. It usually costs less than 50 cents a loaf, depending on the recipe, it may be as low as 35 cents or so. The only drawback is the time it takes. Most breads take about 3 hours because of the rise time. Quick breads are another option. They usually take about an hour. They taste different because they do not use yeast for leavening. Nevertheless, they can be very tasty and a good option. Find recipes by searching the internet or visiting the library for cookbooks.
- Never miss a meal. By staying on schedule you will function better, curb hunger, and avoid overeating.
- Monitor your food staples. When a staple item is half used, then it is time to buy more. Over time you will get a feel for just when more of a staple needs to be purchased.
- Store food properly to retain as many nutrients as possible.
- Use leftovers promptly or freeze them. However you decide to use them, check your refrigerator every two to three days to ensure none are rotting in a back corner.
- Prepare meals ahead of time when you can. Keep enough for a couple of meals in the refrigerator and store the rest in meal-sized portions in the freezer. Mark with the date and contents. Plan to use them within three months.

Shopping strategies

- Plan your menu and draw up a list of needed ingredients. Check your staples to see if you need to restock. Add those items to your list. Shop according to your list.
- If your local Walmart carries groceries, do your food shopping there. We have done comparison shopping between stores (Giant, Safeway, Harris Teeter, Bloom's, Shopper's) and found Walmart's **Great Value** store brand to be the lowest priced.
- Comparison shopping is critical to getting more value for the dollars you have to spend. Compare prices on all the options for a particular item on your list. Make sure you include the store brand. Most store brands are a better value than national brands because they do not pay for advertising. Compare the price per ounce for each brand. This is often listed in small type at the bottom of the shelf tag or you can calculate it by dividing the price by the number of ounces in the package. Do this for each brand and package size to determine the lowest pricing per ounce.
- Normally you can save dollars by buying larger packages. However, it is worth comparing the large to the small. We have found instances of greater savings from buying two smaller packages of the same product.
- Buy in volume if possible. Set up an extended pantry space in a closet or cabinet near the kitchen. Organize it based on the products you use in large amounts. Put in shelves, racks, lazy Susans, and bins. Group like products together. Store items no more than two deep so you can easily find any item. Pay attention to expiration dates and make sure you rotate items with the nearest expiration dates to the front so they get used first.
- When you shop for food look for food that is on sale or the lowest price for that category. Plan your menu around these foods.
- Shop primarily around the perimeter of a grocery store. This is where the majority of fresh, unprocessed foods are. You get more food for your dollar and fewer preservatives and other food additives.
- Coupons can be an asset in your money savings strategy. However, check to be sure there is not a comparable item for even less. Often store brands are cheaper even when the national brand offers a coupon savings.
- Buy plenty of fresh fruits and vegetables. Not only is this better for you, you will also feel fuller and more satisfied by including lots of fruits and vegetables in your diet.
- Wilted and shriveled produce should not have a place in your shopping cart. Examine your intended fruit and vegetable purchases for signs of

decay — bruising, discoloration, wilting, browning, soft spots, depressions, and mold. These items are not as nutritious, will not keep long, and may make you sick.

- Club cards are fine as long as one does not have to pass over currency to get them. There are some cards for which you must pay a fee or membership. Before purchasing these, carefully consider whether or not you will be able to recoup the cost with the savings you may "earn". For many buyers, these cards are not worth the fee.

- Avoid surprises at the checkout counter by taking a calculator with you when you shop. It aids you in keeping track of how much cost you have accumulated while shopping. One strategy is to key in the amount you have to spend and then subtract the amount of each item as it goes into your shopping cart. When the calculator reads near zero, you are done shopping. Do not forget about any tax or surcharge on your groceries. A solar-powered calculator costs only a few dollars and eliminates the need to buy batteries.

- Another helpful tool is a magnifying glass to help you read the ingredient lists on the things you plan to purchase. Always read the ingredients list because manufacturers can change the ingredients at their discretion without getting your approval (imagine!). A magnifier is useful for matching UPC codes to ensure the price you see is for the item you wish to buy. Keep it handy in your pocket or purse.

- Expiration and "use by" dates for all items should be checked before you buy. Check canned goods for dents as the contents of dented cans spoil faster than the contents of un-dented cans.

- The time of day when you shop is important. Try to choose a time when the store has only a few customers. You can take your time in the aisles to compare item prices and ingredients.

- Eat before you shop. If possible never shop when your stomach is grumbling with hunger. You will be tempted to overspend.

- Tell your small children before going shopping that only the things on the list will be allowed in the shopping cart. Have them help you choose items from your prepared list and place them in the cart.

- Keep to your prepared list.

- Ingredients are very important. They can enhance your health or cause it to decline. Take some time to learn about the ingredients that make up your food. Know which ones to accentuate (like whole grains, omega 3 fatty acids, and complex carbohydrates); and which ones to avoid (like hydrogenated oils, high amounts of sugar and salt, cholesterol, and large amounts of saturated fats). Some other names for added sugars include sucrose, glucose, dextrose, maltodextrin, high fructose corn syrup, corn syrup, maple syrup, and fructose. Research shows that eating less than 2,300 milligrams of sodium (about 1 tsp of salt) per day may reduce the risk of high blood pressure. Most of the sodium people eat comes from processed foods, not from the saltshaker. Also look for foods high in potassium, which counteracts some of sodium's effects on blood pressure.

- Shopping bags whether paper, plastic, canvas or other fabric should be kept and reused. Some stores will give you 5¢ or more per bag you reuse. Other stores now charge a fee for each bag they provide. Ask the store manager or cashier what the store's policy is.
- Look for stores which offer double coupon days and have a "price beater" policy where they will beat any advertised price.
- Always choose the most nutritious items which will fit into your budget i.e. whole grain breakfast cereal over high sugar types and dark green lettuces over light green iceberg types.
- Enjoy grocery store samples. Some offer them daily; others during special events.
- Check the internet to see if there is a bakery outlet near you. Search for "Bakery outlet". Expect bargain prices on day-old bread and snack goods.
- Buy cleaning products from dollar stores or Walmart rather than grocery stores.
- Buy the large sizes of dish soap and liquid hand soap. Fill smaller dispensers at the sink. You'll get the discount on the larger size and still have the manageable bottle sizes ready to hand.

Other Ways to Free up Cash

You have more money available for food if your other living expenses are low. Here are some ideas on freeing up cash.

- Consider downsizing your living quarters – you'll save on rent, utilities, decorating, and maintenance.
- Review all of your insurance policies including auto, home, life, and disability. Can you lower your premiums by: switching to another carrier or lowering your deductible? Are there discounts for daylight running lights, multi-car, anti-theft devices, safe driver, home ownership or anything else? For every type of policy you have, ask what discounts are available and see if you qualify. If you do not currently qualify for a discount, check to see if there is something you can alter which will allow you to qualify (install smoke alarms, insure both your auto and home through the same insurer, etc.). Are you paying for insurance

inappropriate to your needs? You only need life insurance if someone is depending on your income (a spouse or child for instance). Most people who need life insurance are best served by term insurance (much less expensive) rather than whole life.

- If you cannot move to smaller quarters consider closing off rooms and their heating ducts to lower your utility bills.
- Get a roommate and share expenses.
- Lower your thermostat in winter (every degree you lower it saves 3% on your energy bill). Wear long johns under your clothes to stay comfortable. Raise the thermostat in summer to save on air conditioning costs.
- Call your utility company to see if they have a program for assisting with utility bills — many do, provided you meet a certain income level.
- After heating and cooling, the next highest energy user is the hot water heater. Insulate the heater and any exposed hot water pipes.
- Most clothes can be washed in cold water with a cold water rinse. You'll save on the utility bill, plus cold water helps fabrics last longer so you don't have to replace clothes as often.
- Install a low-flow showerhead and faucet in the bathroom.
- Take quick showers.
- Turn off the water while you brush your teeth. Just use it to wet the brush and rinse.
- If your work schedule allows, live like the chickens do — up at dawn and to bed by sunset. You'll save on lighting costs.
- Hang insulated drapes in front of the windows.
- Seal windows with weather stripping or plastic sheeting to stop the flow of cold air into the house.
- Search thrift shops for bargain clothing. If you still need some item of clothing check at Walmart, Kmart, and, finally, Target in that order. Consignment shops may also offer good deals on clothing.
- If possible, organically grow fruits and vegetables you enjoy and use most often. Doing this will save you dollars and ensure you have your produce at its peak ripeness, flavor, and nutrient content. Preserving your home-grown produce by canning, freezing, and drying will increase your savings even more.

Free Food Sources

To get more money for food or free food, try the following:

- Visit food banks or pantries. Most have income thresholds. Expect to provide information on your income and expenses and provide proof (like copies of earning statements and bills). Prior to dropping by the food bank, call to find out what documentation you need to bring with you to sign up.

- Contact a local shelter for information about local food assistance programs.
- Apply for food stamps. Additional information on the food stamp program is included in the next section titled "More information on the Supplemental Nutrition Assistance Program (SNAP)".
- If you have children under the age of 5 or a pregnant or nursing woman in the household, you may be eligible for the Women, Infants, and Children (WIC) program which delivers food to your home twice a month. For more information check the United States Department of Agriculture's website for contact information for each state at www.fns.usda/wic.
- Children need the energy provided by a good lunch. Check to see if your family qualifies for the National School Lunch Program. Applying to the National School Lunch Program will also determine eligibility for the School Breakfast Program, the Special Milk Program, the Child and Adult Care Food Program, and the Summer Food Service Program. More information is available at www.fns.usda/cnd.
- Cook at home. Eating out is always more expensive.
- Attend church and school potluck dinners. For the price of the dish you bring, you'll be able to eat a wide range of entrees, side dishes and desserts. If you find a dish you particularly like, ask the cook for the recipe. Side dishes are usually the least expensive option to bring for your contribution. Consider corn bread, green bean casserole, coleslaw, fresh salad, a crudités tray of fresh vegetables or fruits with a dip, potato salad, or a pot of greens.
- Learn to garden. Even people with no yard whatsoever may be able to grow fresh herbs on a windowsill or hang a tomato cage from a bracket attached to the outside wall. Lots of vegetables do well in containers. A small patio could provide space for tomatoes, runner beans grown up a trellis, lettuce, spinach, red cabbage, zucchini (you probably only need one of these they are so productive), and many more. A tiny garden can provide fresh produce throughout the summer and is easy to tend. Grow what you like to eat. Don't waste effort and money on something you will not eat.
- If you know a gardener or farmer, see if you can barter for some of their excess produce. Most gardeners find they have more tomatoes, cucumbers, or zucchini than they can use. Farmers will often allow people to glean their fields after the harvest is collected. Machines used

for harvesting fruits and vegetables often leave useable amounts behind which are not cost effective for the farmer to collect.

- Learn to preserve any extra food so you will have some available later. For instance, if you are able to glean a tomato field, you may have much more fruit than you can use before it spoils. Cut out the part which connects to the plant and freeze the tomatoes with the skin on in freezer bags. The skins will slip off when you let the tomatoes thaw. Then either chop or blend in a blender, pour it in a pot, add some spices, bring it to a boil, then reduce the heat and let it simmer for an hour for tasty tomato sauce to use over noodles.

More information on the Supplemental Nutrition Assistance Program (SNAP)

Qualifying For SNAP

SNAP is a federally funded benefit. Anyone can apply for SNAP. To get SNAP, you and the other people in your household must meet certain economic conditions. Everyone who is applying in your household must have or apply for a Social Security number and be either a U.S. citizen or have a qualified alien status.

To find the local office which processes SNAP eligibility applications, look in the telephone book under "Food Stamps," "Social Services," "Human Services," "Public Assistance," or a similar title or use the Internet search term "SNAP USDA apply". You will be interviewed by a SNAP service representative and will be required to present your driver's license or state identification card, birth certificate or alien card.

Household Income and Resources Requirements

You will also need to demonstrate proof of income such as cancelled checks or pay stubs for each member of your household. Since the allotment of SNAP benefits is usually determined by household income, additional information might be asked of you or the other people claimed under you.

It is advisable to put together an itemized list of your home expenses such as the amount you pay for rent and utilities, and such items as medical bills, child support payments and daycare expenses. Make sure you are as complete as possible and include all sources of income and expenses.

Under the current program, in order to receive SNAP, an applicant's countable resources cannot exceed $2,000. However, the limit jumps to $3,250 if any member of the applicant's household includes a person 60 years of age or who is medically or psychologically disabled. Countable resources include cash, bank accounts, stocks and many other forms of personal and real property. Some resources are excluded like home and lot. Rules for vehicles vary by state.

Income tests do not apply if all members of the household receive Supplemental Security Income (SSI) or benefits under the Temporary Assistance for Needy Families (TANF) program.

Finally, a SNAP applicant may be able to request and obtain immediate processing of their SNAP request. Otherwise most applicants can expect a formal response to their SNAP application request within thirty days.

2012 HHS Poverty Guidelines

2012 HHS Poverty Guidelines			
Persons in Family	48 Contiguous States and D.C.	Alaska	Hawaii
1	$11,170	$13,970	$12,860
2	15,130	18,920	17,410
3	19,090	23,870	21,960
4	23,050	28,820	26,510
5	27,010	33,770	31,060
6	30,970	38,720	35,610
7	34,930	43,670	40,160
8	38,890	48,620	44,710
For each additional person, add	3,960	4,950	4,550

SOURCE: *Federal Register*, Vol. 77, No. 17, January 26, 2012, pp. 4034-4035

Food-related programs using the guidelines or percentage multiples of the guidelines to determine eligibility include Supplemental Nutrition Assistance Program (SNAP) (formerly Food Stamp Program), Special Supplemental Nutrition Program for Women, Infants, and Children (WIC), National School Lunch Program (for free and reduced-price meals only), School Breakfast Program (for free and reduced-price meals only), Child and Adult Care Food Program (for free and reduced-price meals only), and the Expanded Food and Nutrition Education Program.

Menus

School or Work Lunch Ideas

These convenient lunches do not require refrigeration or a microwave. Mayonnaise or Miracle Whip should not be added to sandwiches before lunchtime, because they may spoil without refrigeration. Instead put ketchup, mustard, or both on the sandwich, or include individually packaged servings of mayonnaise. In general do not include any milk product other than sliced cheese unless it will be refrigerated. So **no** cottage cheese, yogurt, or milk unless refrigeration is available.

Fresh lettuce or spinach on the sandwich is a way to add more vegetable matter. If you have a thermos, a vegetable rich-soup can be substituted for the vegetable.

To create variety, toast the sandwich bread. For more variety, crackers can be substituted for bread with the internal sandwich fixings packaged separately. The cheese, meat or peanut butter can be added to the cracker at lunchtime.

Plan to include a sandwich, a vegetable serving, a fruit serving, and milk purchased at the site or taken in a thermos. Select an item from each of the columns below and you will have a nutritionally balanced lunch.

Sandwich	Vegetable	Fruit
Peanut butter and jelly	Carrot sticks	Apple
Cheese	Celery	Orange
Luncheon Meat (bologna, salami, ham, etc.)	Pickles	Banana
Fried Egg	Cucumber sticks	Raisins
Meat Loaf	Broccoli florets	Craisins
Luncheon Meat and Cheese	Green pepper slices	Pear
Hummus	Tomato	Cherries
Cheese	Zucchini sticks	Grapes
		Plum
		Prunes

Add-ons to the lunch could include:

Hard-boiled egg	¼ cup of nuts	A cookie	10 chips (potato, corn, pretzels)

The egg and nuts are good sources of protein which will help stave off hunger. The other two are treats and should be added much less frequently (once or twice a week).

Snack options

1 serving of crackers (read the package to determine serving size) with peanut butter	
¼ cup nuts and ¼ cup dried fruit (raisins, dried cranberries, prunes, etc.)	
1 serving of crackers with 1/3 can of tuna mixed with 1 teaspoon Miracle Whip or mayonnaise, 1 serving carrot or cucumber sticks	
1 serving of pretzels, ¼ cup cottage cheese, 1 serving of fruit	
¼ cup cottage cheese, cucumber slices, 1 serving of crackers	
¼ cup cottage cheese, tomato wedges, 1 slice toast	
1 serving of crackers with 1 slice cheese	½ cup canned fruit
½ cup carrots or other fresh vegetable	Small piece of fresh fruit
4 oz. corn chips and 2 oz. baked beans	8 oz. glass of milk
Small bowl of cereal and ½ cup of milk	8 oz. glass of juice
¼ peanut butter and jelly sandwich	½ cup yogurt, ½ of a banana
¼ cup peanuts, ½ an apple sliced	A hard-boiled egg
½ cup yogurt, 1 serving fresh fruit	Cheese stick, 1 serving of fruit
Celery sticks with peanut butter	

Budget Friendly Healthy 30 Day Menu Plan

The menu shows what each member of the family would be served. A "(2)" denotes two portions. This is an additional serving for individuals wishing to maintain a weight over 150 pounds. For example:

Breakfast: 1 (2) soft-boiled egg(s), 1 (2) slice(s) toast, jelly or jam, 1 cup orange juice

In the above example, two servings of soft-boiled egg instead of one and two slices of toast instead of one in addition to the jelly or jam and the cup of orange juice will help maintain a weight over 150 pounds.

Have water with all meals including snacks. Children should have milk with their lunch and at least one of their snacks. See the School or Work Lunch section for members of your family who will be away from home during lunch.

Use leftovers for another round of the meal the next day or label and freeze them and pull them out at a later date. Many leftovers like vegetables, beans, and some main dishes make welcome additions to home-made soups.

Day 1

Breakfast: 1 (2) soft-boiled egg(s), 1 (2) slice(s) toast, jelly or jam, 1 cup orange juice

Snack: 1 serving of crackers with 1 tablespoon peanut butter

Lunch: 1 cup Hearty Soup, cheese sandwich made with 1 (2) slice(s) of bread, 1 serving fruit

Snack: ½ cup yogurt, ½ of a banana

Dinner: 1 cup Chunky Bean Chili, 1 slice cornbread, 1 cup cucumber salad (slice cucumbers add a drizzle of your favorite salad dressing), ½ of a medium or large apple sliced

Day 2

Breakfast: 1 cup dry cereal, 1 cup milk, 1 (2) slice(s) toast, ½ (1 full) banana, 1 cup orange juice

Snack: 1 slice of cheese, 1 serving fruit

Lunch: 1 cup Hearty Soup, 1 serving crackers, 1 tablespoon peanut butter, 1 serving fruit

Snack: ½ cup carrots or other fresh vegetable

Dinner: ½ cup (1 cup) Aloha Sautéed Chicken, ½ cup (1 cup) Rice, ½ cup Broccoli, ½ cup canned fruit

Day 3

Breakfast: 1 (2) fried egg(s), milk, 1 (2) slice(s) toast, 1 cup orange juice, jelly

Snack: ¼ cup nuts and ¼ cup dried fruit (raisins, dried cranberries, prunes, etc.)

Lunch: 1 cup Hearty Soup, 1 serving cottage cheese, 1 (2) slice(s) toast, 1 serving fruit

Snack: ½ cup carrots or other fresh vegetable

Dinner: Open-Faced Tuna Melts, tomato wedges, 1 serving fruit

Day 4

Breakfast: 1 serving oatmeal, 5 prunes, 1 cup milk, 1 cup orange juice

Snack: ¼ cup cottage cheese, tomato wedges, 1 serving crackers

Lunch: 1 cup Hearty Soup, 1 serving yogurt, 1 (2) slice(s) toast, 1 serving fruit

Snack: Celery sticks with peanut butter

Dinner: Ramen with a poached egg and 1 serving green beans cooked with the noodles, 1 serving fruit

Day 5

Breakfast: 1 (2) egg(s) scrambled, 1 (2) slice(s) toast, jelly, 1 cup milk, 1 cup orange juice
Snack: ½ cup yogurt, ½ of a banana
Lunch: 1 cup Hearty Soup, 1 peanut butter and jelly sandwich, 1 serving fruit
Snack: 1 serving of crackers with 1 slice cheese
Dinner: Broiled burgers, micro-waved baked sweet potatoes, carrot sticks, celery sticks, 1 serving fruit

Day 6

Breakfast: Cream of wheat, 1 (2) slice(s) toast, jelly, 1 cup milk, 1 cup orange juice
Snack: ¼ cup nuts and ¼ cup dried fruit (raisins, dried cranberries, prunes, etc.)
Lunch: 1 cup Hearty Soup, 1 (2) serving(s) crackers, 1 slice cheese, 1 serving fruit
Snack: 4 oz. corn chips and 2 oz. baked beans
Dinner: Egg salad sandwiches, pickles, tomato slices, apple slices with cinnamon

Day 7

Breakfast: French toast, syrup, 1 cup milk, 1 cup orange juice
Snack: ½ cup yogurt, 1 serving fresh fruit
Lunch: 1 cup Hearty Soup, fried luncheon meat sandwich with ketchup and mustard, 1 serving fruit
Snack: ½ cup carrots or other fresh vegetable
Dinner: Boston Baked Beans, corn bread, coleslaw, pickles, 1 serving fruit

Day 8

Breakfast: Soft-boiled egg(s), 1 (2) slice(s) toast, 1 cup orange juice
Snack: ¼ cup peanuts, ½ an apple sliced
Lunch: 1 cup Hearty Soup, 1 serving cottage cheese, 1 (2) slice(s) toast, 1 serving fruit
Snack: ½ cup canned fruit
Dinner: Macaroni and cheese served over broccoli, 1 serving fruit

Day 9

Breakfast: Grits, 1 (2) slice(s) toast, milk, orange juice
Snack: A hard-boiled egg
Lunch: 1 cup Hearty Soup, cheese sandwich made with 1 (2) slice(s) of bread, 1 serving fruit
Snack: ¼ cup peanuts, ½ an apple sliced
Dinner: 4 oz. pot roast, ½ cup (1 cup) couscous, 1 serving peas, sweet pepper slices, 1 serving fruit

Day 10

Breakfast: Fried egg, 1 (2) slice(s) toast, jelly, milk, orange juice
Snack: ½ cup yogurt, 1 serving fresh fruit
Lunch: 1 cup Hearty Soup, 1 (2) serving(s) crackers, 1 (2) tablespoon(s) peanut butter, 1 serving fruit
Snack: ¼ cup cottage cheese, cucumber slices, 1 serving of bread
Dinner: Sardines on ½ cup (1 cup) rice with 2 servings Oriental Stir-fried vegetables, 1 serving fruit

Day 11

Breakfast: 1 serving oatmeal, 5 prunes, 1 cup milk, 1 cup orange juice
Snack: ¼ cup nuts and ¼ cup dried fruit (raisins, dried cranberries, prunes, etc.)
Lunch: 1 cup Hearty Soup, 1 (2) serving(s) luncheon meat, 1 (2) serving(s) crackers, 1 serving fruit
Snack: ½ cup carrots or other fresh vegetable with ½ cup plain yogurt
Dinner: Baked Ziti with spinach, tomato sauce and cheese, celery sticks, 1 serving fruit

Day 12

Breakfast: 1 (2) egg(s) scrambled, 1 (2) slice(s) toast, jelly, 1 cup milk, 1 cup orange juice
Snack: Celery sticks with peanut butter
Lunch: 1 cup Hearty Soup, 1 serving cheese, 1 (2) slice(s) cornbread, 1 serving fruit
Snack: 1 serving of pretzels, ¼ cup cottage cheese, 1 serving of fruit
Dinner: Beef Stroganoff, 1 (2) serving(s) noodles, 2 servings broccoli, 1 serving fruit

Day 13

Breakfast: Cream of wheat, 1 (2) slice(s) toast, jelly, 1 cup milk, 1 cup orange juice
Snack: ½ cup yogurt, ½ of a banana
Lunch: 1 cup Hearty Soup, cheese sandwich made with 1 (2) slice(s) of bread, 1 serving fruit
Snack: ¼ peanut butter and jelly sandwich
Dinner: Huevos Rancheros, 1 serving corn bread, 1 serving fruit

Day 14

Breakfast: French toast, syrup, 1 cup milk, 1 cup orange juice
Snack: ½ cup yogurt, 1 serving fresh fruit
Lunch: 1 cup Hearty Soup, fried luncheon meat sandwich with ketchup and mustard, 1 serving fruit
Snack: ½ cup carrots or other fresh vegetable
Dinner: Pinto Beans and Rice, salad, 1 serving fruit cocktail

Day 15

Breakfast: Soft-boiled egg, 1 (2) slice(s) toast, 1 cup orange juice
Snack: ¼ cup peanuts, ½ an apple sliced
Lunch: 1 cup Hearty Soup, 1 (2) serving(s) cheese, 1 (2) slice(s) crackers, 1 serving fruit
Snack: Small piece of fresh fruit, 4 oz. glass of milk
Dinner: Gourmet Goulash, 1 (2) serving(s) bread, 2 servings carrot sticks, 1 serving fruit

Day 16

Breakfast: 1 cup dry cereal, 1 cup milk, 1 (2) slice(s) toast, ½ (1 full) banana, 1 cup orange juice
Snack: ¼ cup peanuts, ½ an apple sliced
Lunch: 1 cup Hearty Soup, 1 serving cottage cheese, 1 (2) slice(s) toast, 1 serving fruit
Snack: Hard-boiled egg
Dinner: Chicken Italiano, 1 serving fruit

Day 17

Breakfast: Fried egg, 1 (2) slice(s) toast, jelly, milk, orange juice
Snack: Celery sticks with peanut butter
Lunch: 1 cup Hearty Soup, 1 serving cheese, 1 (2) slice(s) cornbread, 1 serving fruit
Snack: 1 serving of pretzels, ¼ cup cottage cheese, 1 serving of fruit
Dinner: Fish sticks, rice, 2 servings stir-fried vegetables, 1 serving fruit

Day 18

Breakfast: 1 serving oatmeal, 5 prunes, 1 cup milk, 1 cup orange juice
Snack: ¼ cup cottage cheese, tomato wedges, 1 serving crackers
Lunch: 1 cup Hearty Soup, 1 serving yogurt, 1 (2) slice(s) toast, 1 serving fruit
Snack: ¼ cup nuts and ¼ cup dried fruit (raisins, dried cranberries, prunes, etc.)
Dinner: Cheesy Florentine Noodles, 1 cup cucumber slices with a dash of apple cider vinegar and pepper, 1 serving fruit

Day 19

Breakfast: 1 (2) egg(s) scrambled, 1 (2) slice(s) toast, jelly, 1 cup milk, 1 cup orange juice
Snack: ¼ cup nuts and ¼ cup dried fruit (raisins, dried cranberries, prunes, etc.)
Lunch: 1 cup Hearty Soup, 1 serving cottage cheese, 1 (2) serving(s) crackers, 1 serving fruit
Snack: 1 cup cereal and ½ cup of milk
Dinner: Asian Ground Beef and Vegetables, ½ cup (1 cup) rice, ½ cup grapes

Day 20

Breakfast: Cream of wheat, 1 (2) slice(s) toast, jelly, 1 cup milk, 1 cup orange juice
Snack: Small piece of fresh fruit
Lunch: 1 cup Hearty Soup, fried luncheon meat sandwich with ketchup and mustard, 1 serving fruit
Snack: ¼ peanut butter and jelly sandwich, 4 oz. milk
Dinner: Mushroom and broccoli omelettes, lettuce with shredded carrot, tomato slices, baked apples

Day 21

Breakfast: French toast, syrup, 1 cup milk, 1 cup orange juice
Snack: ½ cup yogurt, 1 serving fresh fruit
Lunch: 1 cup Hearty Soup, grilled cheese sandwich with ketchup, 1 serving fruit
Snack: ¼ cup nuts and ¼ cup dried fruit (raisins, dried cranberries, prunes, etc.)
Dinner: Bean Casserole, 1 cup raw mixed vegetables (for example: carrot, celery, or cucumber sticks, grape tomatoes, cauliflower or broccoli florets), 1 serving crackers, apple slices

Day 22

Breakfast: Soft-boiled egg, 1 (2) slice(s) toast, 1 cup orange juice
Snack: ¼ cup peanuts, ½ an apple sliced
Lunch: 1 cup Hearty Soup, 1 (2) serving(s) cheese, 1 (2) slice(s) crackers, 1 serving fruit
Snack: Small piece of fresh fruit, 4 oz. glass of milk
Dinner: Cottage Cheese Relish served in tomato cups, crackers with spread and jelly, 1 serving fruit

Day 23

Breakfast: 1 cup dry cereal, 1 cup milk, 1 (2) slice(s) toast, ½ (1 full) banana, 1 cup orange juice
Snack: ¼ cup peanuts, ½ an apple sliced
Lunch: 1 cup Hearty Soup, 1 tuna fish sandwich, 1 serving fruit
Snack: ½ cup carrots or other fresh vegetable with ½ cup plain yogurt
Dinner: Turkey Sausage Casserole, 1 serving green beans, ½ cup carrot sticks, 1 serving fruit

Day 24

Breakfast: Fried egg, 1 (2) slice(s) toast, jelly, milk, orange juice
Snack: Celery sticks with peanut butter
Lunch: 1 cup Hearty Soup, 1 serving cheese, 1 (2) slice(s) cornbread, 1 serving fruit
Snack: 1 serving of pretzels, ¼ cup yogurt, 1 serving of fruit
Dinner: Pink Salmon with Pineapple Brown Sugar Rice, sautéed onions and green beans, 1 serving fruit

Day 25

Breakfast: 1 serving oatmeal, 5 prunes, 1 cup milk, 1 cup orange juice
Snack: ¼ cup cottage cheese, tomato wedges, 1 serving crackers
Lunch: 1 cup Hearty Soup, 1 serving yogurt, 1 (2) slice(s) toast, 1 serving fruit
Snack: ¼ cup nuts and ¼ cup dried fruit (raisins, dried cranberries, prunes, etc.)
Dinner: Spaghetti with Pepperoni Sauce, 1 slice garlic bread, ½ cup celery sticks, 1 serving grapes

Day 26

Breakfast: 1 (2) egg(s) scrambled, 1 (2) slice(s) toast, jelly, 1 cup milk, 1 cup orange juice
Snack: ¼ cup nuts and ¼ cup dried fruit (raisins, dried cranberries, prunes, etc.)
Lunch: 1 cup Hearty Soup, 1 serving cottage cheese, 1 (2) serving(s) crackers, 1 serving fruit
Snack: 1 cup cereal and ½ cup of milk
Dinner: Sloppy Joe's sauce on bread, burger bun, or roll, ½ cup pepper slices, 1 serving coleslaw, 1 serving fruit

Day 27

Breakfast: Cream of wheat, 1 (2) slice(s) toast, jelly, 1 cup milk, 1 cup orange juice
Snack: Small piece of fresh fruit
Lunch: 1 cup Hearty Soup, fried luncheon meat sandwich with ketchup and mustard, 1 serving fruit
Snack: ¼ peanut butter and jelly sandwich, 4 oz. milk
Dinner: Western Omelette, Baked Potato, 1 serving fruit

Day 28

Breakfast: French toast, syrup, 1 cup milk, 1 cup orange juice
Snack: ½ cup yogurt, 1 serving fresh fruit
Lunch: 1 cup Hearty Soup, grilled cheese sandwich with ketchup, 1 serving fruit
Snack: ¼ cup nuts and ¼ cup dried fruit (raisins, dried cranberries, prunes, etc.)
Dinner: Seasoned Baked Beans, Rice, ½ cup carrot slices, ½ an apple sliced

Day 29

Breakfast: Soft-boiled egg, 1 (2) slice(s) toast, 1 cup orange juice
Snack: ¼ cup peanuts, ½ an apple sliced
Lunch: 1 cup Hearty Soup, 1 (2) slice(s) cheese, 1 (2) serving(s) crackers, 1 serving fruit
Snack: Small piece of fresh fruit, 4 oz. glass of milk
Dinner: Potato Pancakes, ½ cup applesauce, slice of cheese, crudités, ½ cup fruit cocktail

Day 30

Breakfast: 1 cup dry cereal, 1 cup milk, 1 (2) slice(s) toast, ½ (1 full) banana, 1 cup orange juice
Snack: ¼ cup peanuts, ½ an apple sliced
Lunch: 1 cup Hearty Soup, 1 tuna fish sandwich, 1 serving fruit
Snack: ½ cup carrots or other fresh vegetable with ½ cup plain yogurt
Dinner: Tender Herbed Chicken, ½ cup (1 cup) Fluffy Orange Rice, ½ cup broccoli, ½ an orange sliced

Austerity Eating for $28 a week (or $4 a day)

If the cupboards are bare and your wallet is thin, here is a six-week austerity-eating plan to keep your family of four going until you get a new source of income or visit the food bank.

This menu plan is based on low-cost, wholesome foods. We provide this plan with four provisions.

First, food prices shift constantly, usually upward. Depending on where you live and the stores which are available to you, food prices might be different from the ones listed in this book. You may even be able to find better pricing on some items or lower the prices with coupons. However, generally speaking these items will be the least expensive food items whatever the economy. We have included the pricing of items based on a recent visit to a Walmart Supercenter. We chose Walmart for this example because they have stores in all fifty states and fifteen countries overseas at the time of this writing. So it is likely you will find a Walmart near you.

You will be able to provide more food by using the School Lunch Program, visiting the Food Bank, applying for the Food Stamp Program and the Women, Infant, and Children (WIC) Program as applicable to your situation.

Second, this six week menu assumes you have absolutely nothing in your refrigerator or pantry, not even salt. More likely you have a few things on hand; perhaps spices, a few condiments, a can of this or that. If so, skip buying that item if it is suggested below, and spend the savings on an item from the next week's suggested additional purchase list.

Third, these menus are compiled with adults in mind. If you have very young children, they may not need to eat as much as an adult, and therefore, the adults may divide the surplus.

Fourth, this plan does not meet the USDA recommended daily amounts for adults, particularly in the first couple of weeks, although it does meet the variety spread. You may lose weight on this diet. As time goes on, you will be able to get closer to the recommended calorie intake as you will see in the later weeks of the plan when you build up your pantry and have more food available.

Portion sizes are very important in meeting both the nutritional and budgetary goals. Measure each serving to maximize the food value for each person and stretch the food until the end of the week.

Breakfast per person:
1 serving of oatmeal
1 serving milk
1 serving orange juice

Lunch per person:
1 serving sliced white bread (toast it if you like)
1 cup soup (see the Easy Vegetable Soup Recipe below)
½ of a small apple

Easy Vegetable Soup recipe:
1 lb vegetable from a 5 lb package of Frozen Mixed Vegetables
½ of a 32 oz. can of Spaghetti Sauce
1 lb frozen ground turkey
Salt to taste
Water

1. Brown turkey in an 8-quart sauce pan.
2. Stir in half a cup water and rub the flavorful browning on the bottom of the pan.
3. Add the pound of vegetables, the spaghetti sauce, salt, and enough water to bring the mixture to within 1 inch of the pot brim. Stir.
4. Bring to a boil. Turn down heat and simmer for ½ an hour. Turn off heat. Serving size = 1 cup.

Dinner per person:
1 serving rice
1 serving pinto beans, cooked with 1 lb mixed vegetables (see notes below)
1 serving apple sauce

Cook ½ of the rice per the instructions on the bag. You will use this rice down the week. Save the rest of the rice for next week.

Note: Purchase dry pinto beans instead of canned since this is the least expensive way to buy them. Cook them yourself. Follow the directions on the package. In the last ½ hour of cooking, add the pound of frozen vegetables.

Purchase List for Week 1:

Quantity	Size	Item	Price per unit	Total Cost
2	gallon	Milk	$2.52	$5.12
1	32 oz.	Oatmeal	$2.28	$2.28
4	10 oz.	Orange juice frozen	$1.14	$4.56
1	loaf	White bread	$1.08	$1.08
1	1 lb	Ground turkey frozen	$1.00	$1.00
1	3 lb bag	Apples	$4.47	$4.47
1	1 lb bag	Pinto beans	$0.68	$0.68
1	32 oz.	Apple sauce	$1.46	$1.46
1	5 lb bag	Mixed Vegetables frozen	$3.77	$3.77
1	32 oz. can	Spaghetti sauce	$0.98	$0.98
1	5 lb bag	Rice	$2.68	$2.68
1	package	Salt	$0.33	$0.33
		Weekly Total		**$28.41**

*Remember — pricing may have changed so you may have to adjust what you purchase and serve. Keep these ideas in mind:

1. Have protein with each meal. Milk, beans, peanut butter, peanuts, and meat are all good sources. Protein is usually the most expensive part of a meal. Substitute beans for meat if you need to. Make the soup with beans or, if beans are high, try adding peanut butter to the bread and omit the protein in the soup.

2. If the pricing on the large size bags of vegetables or rice breaks the budget, see if you can purchase smaller quantities which give you enough for the week but perhaps do not provide the same carryover to the following week. It will take you longer to reach a more diverse diet, but you will be able to feed your family.

3. We have used orange juice and apple sauce in this example but you could use ½ piece of fruit for each of their respective servings instead. Use your comparative shopping skills to determine which is cheaper. For this diet you will need a total of 84 fruit servings for the week. Check the pricing on bananas, oranges, apples, and so on to find the best deal.

Week 2:

Breakfast per person:
1 serving of oatmeal
1 serving milk
1 serving orange juice

Lunch per person:
1 serving sliced white bread
1 cup soup
½ of a small apple

Dinner per person:
1 serving rice
1 serving pinto beans, cooked with 1 pound mixed vegetables (see notes below)
1 serving apple sauce

Carried over from last week:

3 pounds of frozen mixed vegetables	2 ½ pounds of rice
2 servings of oatmeal	4 servings of milk

Purchase List for Week 2:

Quantity	Size	Item	Price per unit	Total Cost
2	gallon	Milk	$2.52	$5.12
1	32 oz.	Oatmeal	$2.28	$2.28
4	10 oz.	Orange juice frozen	$1.14	$4.56
1	loaf	White bread	$1.08	$1.08
1	1 lb	Ground turkey frozen	$1.00	$1.00
1	3 lb bag	Apples	$4.47	$4.47
1	1 lb bag	Pinto beans	$0.68	$0.68
1	32 oz.	Apple sauce	$1.46	$1.46
1	dozen	Eggs	$1.57	$1.57
1	5 lb bag	Flour	$1.74	$1.74
1	5 lb bag	Sugar	$2.54	$2.54
2	5 ½ oz.	Tuna	$0.60	$1.20
1	package	Ramen noodles	$0.17	$0.17
		Weekly Total		**$27.87**

Week 3:

Breakfast per person:
1 serving of oatmeal (Can add sugar to oatmeal.)
1 serving milk
1 serving orange juice

Lunch per person:
1 serving sliced white bread (toast it if you like)
1 cup soup
½ of a small apple
Add a hard-boiled egg on 2 days. Add 1 tablespoon peanut butter on 2 days.

Dinner per person:
1 serving rice
1 serving pinto beans, cooked with 1 pound mixed vegetables
1 serving apple sauce
Add 1 serving of milk on 2 days.

Carried over from last week:

1 pound of frozen mixed vegetables	1 package Ramen	4 eggs
4 servings of milk	Flour	Sugar
4 servings of oatmeal		

Purchase List for Week 3:

Quantity	Size	Item	Price per unit	Total Cost
2	gallon	Milk	$2.52	$5.12
1	32 oz.	Oatmeal	$2.28	$2.28
4	10 oz.	Orange juice frozen	$1.14	$4.56
1	loaf	White bread	$1.08	$1.08
1	32 oz. can	Spaghetti sauce	$0.98	$0.98
1	1 lb	Ground turkey frozen	$1.00	$1.00
1	3 lb bag	Apples	$4.47	$4.47
1	5 lb bag	Rice	$2.68	$2.68
1	1 lb bag	Pinto beans	$0.68	$0.68
1	32 oz.	Apple sauce	$1.46	$1.46
1	Dozen	Eggs	$1.57	$1.57
1	28 oz.	Peanut Butter	$2.56	$2.56
		Weekly Total		**$28.44**

Week 4:

Breakfast per person:
1 serving of oatmeal (Can add sugar to oatmeal.)
1 serving milk
1 serving orange juice

Lunch per person:
1 serving sliced white bread (toast it if you like)
1 cup soup
½ of a small apple
Add a hard-boiled egg on 2 days. Add 1 tablespoon peanut butter on 2 days.

Dinner per person:
1 serving rice
1 serving pinto beans, cooked with 1 pound mixed vegetables
1 serving apple sauce
Add 1 serving of milk on 1 day.

Carried over from last week:

2 ½ lbs rice	20 oz. peanut butter
1 package Ramen	4 servings of milk
6 servings of oatmeal	8 eggs
Flour	Sugar

Purchase List for Week 4:

Quantity	Size	Item	Price per unit	Total Cost
2	gallon	Milk	$2.52	$5.12
1	32 oz.	Oatmeal	$2.28	$2.28
4	10 oz.	Orange juice frozen	$1.14	$4.56
1	loaf	White bread	$1.08	$1.08
1	1 lb	Ground turkey frozen	$1.00	$1.00
1	3 lb bag	Apples	$4.47	$4.47
1	1 lb bag	Pinto beans	$0.68	$0.68
1	32 oz.	Apple sauce	$1.46	$1.46
1	48 oz.	Vegetable Oil	$2.78	$2.78
1	1 lb 8 oz.	Corn meal	$1.06	$1.06
		Weekly Total		**$28.26**

Week 5:

Breakfast per person:
1 serving of oatmeal* (Can add sugar to oatmeal.)
1 serving milk
1 serving orange juice
*Have corn meal mush on 2 days. The recipe is on the canister.

Lunch per person:
1 serving sliced white bread (toast it if you like)
1 cup soup
½ of a small apple
Add a hard-boiled egg on 2 days.
Add 1 tablespoon peanut butter on 2 days.
Substitute corn bread for white bread on 3 days. Corn bread recipe is on the canister.

Dinner per person:
1 serving rice
1 serving pinto beans, cooked with 1 pound mixed vegetables
1 serving apple sauce
Add 1 serving of milk on 2 day.

Carried over from last week:

3 lbs mixed vegetables	12 oz. peanut butter
1 package Ramen	4 servings of milk
8 servings of oatmeal	4 eggs
Flour	Sugar
Corn Meal	Vegetable Oil

Purchase List for Week 5:

Quantity	Size	Item	Price per unit	Total Cost
2	gallon	Milk	$2.52	$5.12
1	32 oz.	Oatmeal	$2.28	$2.28
4	10 oz.	Orange juice frozen	$1.14	$4.56
1	loaf	White bread	$1.08	$1.08
1	32 oz. can	Spaghetti sauce	$0.98	$0.98
1	1 lb	Ground turkey frozen	$1.00	$1.00
1	3 lb bag	Apples	$4.47	$4.47
1	5 lb bag	Rice	$2.68	$2.68
1	1 lb bag	Pinto beans	$0.68	$0.68
1	32 oz.	Apple sauce	$1.46	$1.46
1	Dozen	Eggs	$1.57	$1.57
1	10 oz. can	Baking Powder	$1.04	$1.04
1	1 lb	Noodles	$1.00	$1.00
		Weekly Total		**$27.92**

Week 6:

Breakfast per person:
1 serving of oatmeal or corn mush*
1 serving milk
1 serving orange juice
*Have oatmeal on 4 days and corn meal mush on 3 days. Add sugar to oatmeal or corn mush if desired.
Add an egg on 2 days.

Mid-Morning Snack:
Have a ½ slice of toast per person for 5 days.

Lunch per person:
1 serving sliced white bread (toast it if you like)
1 cup soup
½ of a small apple
Add 1 tablespoon peanut butter on 1 day.
Add corn bread on 3 days.

Afternoon Snack:
Have ½ of a package of cooked ramen noodles with the broth and ½ of a hard-boiled egg per person on 2 days.

Dinner per person:
1 serving rice*
1 serving Pinto Beans, cooked with 1 pound mixed vegetables
1 serving Apple Sauce
*Have Easy Cheesy Noodle casserole with Simple Dinner Rolls on 2 days in place of the rice and pinto beans. Recipes follow.

Easy Cheesy Noodle Casserole recipe:
1 (16 oz.) box noodles
1 (32 oz.) can spaghetti sauce
½ of a 16 oz. container of cottage cheese

Preheat oven to 350 degrees. Cook one 1 lb package of noodles of any type according to the directions. Drain noodles and spread in a 9- X 13-inch baking dish. Pour a 32 oz. can of spaghetti sauce over the noodles and stir. Spoon ½ of a 16 oz. container of cottage cheese over the mixed noodles and sauce. Bake for 45 minutes. Remove foil and bake 10 more minutes. Makes 8 servings.

Simple Dinner Rolls

3 cups flour

2 tablespoons sugar

2 teaspoons yeast

1 teaspoon salt (optional)

1 cups + 2 tablespoons warm water (115°-125°F)

2 tablespoons oil

Measure and place all dry ingredients in large mixing bowl. Make a well in the center. Pour water and oil into the well. Mix slowly with a spoon until all dry ingredients are incorporated. Oil another large bowl. Place the dough ball in the oiled bowl; cover with a clean dish cloth and leave to rise to double its size (about 2 hours) in a warm place. Flour a sheet of wax paper or the countertop. Place the dough on the surface and knead until the size of the dough is reduced by roughly half. Roll the dough out in a log. Break off handful size pieces from the log. Roll each piece into a ball and place in an oiled baking pan (8 or 9 inch round cake pans work well). Cover with a clean dish cloth and allow to rise until double their size. Bake in a 350° oven until lightly browned about 20 minutes. Serving size = 1 roll.

Carried over from last week:

1 lb mixed vegetables	4 oz. peanut butter
1 package Ramen	4 servings of milk
18 servings of oatmeal	8 eggs
2 ½ lbs rice	10 slices of bread
Flour	Sugar
Corn Meal	Vegetable Oil

Purchase List for Week 6:

Quantity	Size	Item	Price per unit	Total Cost
2	gallon	Milk	$2.52	$5.12
4	10 oz.	Orange juice frozen	$1.14	$4.56
1	loaf	White bread	$1.08	$1.08
3	32 oz. can	Spaghetti sauce	$0.98	$2.94
1	1 lb	Ground turkey frozen	$1.00	$1.00
1	3 lb bag	Apples	$4.47	$4.47
1	1 lb bag	Pinto beans	$0.68	$0.68
1	32 oz.	Apple sauce	$1.46	$1.46
1	28 oz.	Peanut Butter	$2.56	$2.56
1	16 oz.	Cottage Cheese	$1.98	$1.98
1	Dozen	Eggs	$1.57	$1.57
3	package	Ramen noodles	$0.17	$0.51
4	packets	Yeast	$1.02	$1.02
1	1 lb	Noodles	$1.00	$1.00
		Weekly Total		**$27.97**

Appendix A: Recipes

Aloha Sautéed Chicken

2 chicken breasts, cut into ½-inch cubes
1 medium onion, sliced
1 (15 oz.) can pineapple chunks, drained
(save the juice)

1 teaspoon soy sauce
¼ teaspoon thyme
1 tablespoon lemon juice

Sauté chicken in oil stirring frequently until cooked. When chicken is cooked (no longer pink inside), add sliced onions to oil. Cook until translucent, about 5 minutes. Add drained pineapple to pan. Stir frequently. Cook until lightly browned. Add ½ cup pineapple juice, soy sauce, thyme, and lemon juice to pan. Cook 5 more minutes over low heat. Stir constantly. Serves four.

Asian Ground Beef and Vegetables

1 lb ground beef (or ground turkey, if you prefer)
2 tablespoons sesame oil
1 medium onion, sliced
1 green bell pepper, sliced
1 large carrot, sliced on a slant

1 cup frozen green beans
½ cup frozen corn
2 large cloves garlic, thinly sliced
2 teaspoons sesame seeds
2 tablespoons soy sauce

Brown the beef or turkey in a large skillet over medium heat. Use a spatula to stir ingredients as they cook. Add the onion and pepper. Cook until onion is translucent. Add remaining vegetables including garlic. Raise heat to medium high. Cook until vegetables are tender and lightly browned. Add sesame seeds and soy sauce. Turn off heat. Serve over rice, noodles, or couscous. Serves four.

Cheesy Florentine Noodles

3 ounces extra wide noodles (or ruffle noodles work well too)
4 cups packed, shredded fresh spinach leaves or 1 (10 oz.) package thawed frozen spinach
1 (15 oz.) can tomato sauce
1 small garlic clove, minced

¼ teaspoon dried basil
¼ teaspoon dried oregano
2 tablespoons onions, finely chopped
1 ¼ cups cottage cheese
¾ cup shredded mozzarella cheese
¼ teaspoon salt (optional)
Cooking spray

Cook noodles in boiling water until just tender to bite (about 5 to 7 minutes). Drain; rinse with hot water. While cooking noodles, steam the spinach for 5 minutes and drain in a sieve. Press with a spoon to remove excess moisture. In a 10-inch skillet coated lightly with cooking spray, cook onion until tender. Stir in spinach. Cook until excess moisture evaporates. Remove from heat. Add tomato sauce, garlic, basil, oregano, cottage cheese and salt if desired. Stir mixture together. Spread ½ of noodles in a 2-quart casserole dish. Spoon half of the spinach-tomato sauce filling over the noodles. Spread the remaining noodles over the filling and then spread the remaining spinach-tomato sauce over the noodles. Sprinkle the mozzarella cheese over the top. Cover with aluminum foil. Bake in a 350° oven for 45 minutes. Remove foil and bake an additional 10 minutes or until cheese is bubbly and lightly browned. Makes 8 servings.

Chicken Italiano

1 cup rice
6 chicken tenderloins or 2 breasts, halved
2 cups spaghetti sauce

1 cup green beans (or broccoli)
½ cup mozzarella cheese

Mix rice, green beans, and 1½ cups spaghetti sauce in 9- X 11-inch baking pan. Lay chicken on top of rice mixture. Pour remaining spaghetti sauce over chicken. Sprinkle mozzarella cheese over the top. Cover with aluminum foil. Bake one hour at 350°. Remove foil. Bake an additional 15 minutes or until cheese is bubbly and lightly browned. Serves four.

Chunky Bean Chili

1 medium onion, chopped
1 bell pepper, chopped
1 (32 oz.) can of chopped tomatoes
1 (15 oz.) can of dark kidney beans
1 (15 oz.) can of light kidney beans

2 cloves garlic, minced
2 teaspoon chili powder
2 teaspoon paprika
¼ teaspoon black pepper
¼ teaspoon red pepper flakes (optional)

Sauté onions until translucent, about 5 minutes, in a large sauce pan. Add bell pepper and cook until tender. Add remaining ingredients. Stir. Bring to a boil, reduce heat and simmer 30 minutes to meld flavors. Serving size = 1 cup.

Confetti Cottage Cheese Relish

1½ cups cottage cheese
¼ cup onion, chopped and sautéed
¼ cup frozen whole corn

¼ cup green peppers, chopped
¼ cup carrots, chopped
Black pepper to taste

Cook the onion and corn in a skillet until onions are translucent. Mix cottage cheese and vegetables. Serve in 4 tomato cups or 4 portions with tomato slices. Sprinkle with black pepper.

Easy Cheesy Noodle Casserole

1 (16 oz.) box noodles
1 (32 oz.) can spaghetti sauce

8 oz. cottage cheese

Preheat oven to 350°. Cook one 1 lb package of noodles of any type according to the directions. Drain noodles and spread in a 9- X 13-inch baking dish. Pour a 32 oz. can of spaghetti sauce over the noodles and stir. Spoon the 8 oz. container of cottage cheese over the mixed noodles and sauce. Cover with foil and bake for 45 minutes. Remove foil and bake 10 more minutes. Makes 8 servings.

Easy Vegetable Soup

1 lb frozen mixed vegetables
1 (16 oz.) Spaghetti Sauce
1 lb frozen ground turkey

1 tablespoon salt
Water

Brown turkey in an 8-quart sauce pan. Stir in ½ cup of water and dislodge the flavorful browning on the bottom of the pan. Add the pound of vegetables, the spaghetti sauce, salt, and enough water to bring the mixture to within 1 inch of the pot brim. Stir. Bring to a boil. Turn down heat and simmer for half an hour. Stir occasionally. Turn off heat. Serving size = 1 cup.

Fluffy Orange Rice

1 cup celery, chopped
¼ cup onion, chopped
Cooking spray or light coating of oil
2 tablespoons orange-juice concentrate

2 cups water
½ teaspoon salt (optional)
1 cup rice

Cook celery and onion in skillet until tender. Stir in rice to pick up any remaining oil. Add concentrate, water, and salt. Stir to mix. Bring to a boil. Reduce heat and let simmer for 25 minutes. Remove from heat and let rest 5 minutes. The bottom of the rice should be slightly brown from the pan juices. Serves four.

Gourmet Goulash

1 lb ground beef (or ground turkey)
1 cup onion, chopped
1 clove garlic, crushed
1 teaspoon salt (optional)
3 cups noodles (any shape noodle will do)
2 ½ cups tomato juice
1 ½ teaspoons Worcestershire sauce
1 teaspoon salt (optional)

Dash pepper
1 can condensed beef broth (or 1 cube bouillon in 1 cup water)
½ cup water
1/3 cup chopped green pepper
1 cup dairy sour cream
1 (3 oz.) can sliced mushrooms

Brown beef, onion, garlic, and 1 teaspoon salt, if desired, in oiled skillet. Add noodles. Combine next six ingredients and pour over noodles. Cover. Bring to a boil and immediately reduce temperature to a simmer. Cook 20 minutes, stirring occasionally. Add green pepper. Cover and cook 10 minutes or till noodles are tender. Stir in mushrooms and sour cream. Heat through and serve. Serving size = 1 cup.

Hearty Soup

1 lb ground turkey (frozen is fine)
1 small onion
½ can of tomato sauce (about 7 oz.), or tomato soup, or fresh chopped or pureed tomatoes (freeze any extra for use in next week's soup)
½ cup dry noodles any type
1 teaspoon basil

1 teaspoon oregano
1 cup potatoes or sweet potatoes, ½-inch cubes
3 cups chopped vegetables any type, in any combination for a total of 3 cups (green beans, corn, carrots, peppers, greens, etc.)
2 bouillon cubes or 2 teaspoons salt
Water

In a large pot, brown ground turkey. Add onions and sauté until translucent. Add ½ cup water and dislodge the flavorful browning on the bottom of the pan. Add all other ingredients. Add enough water to bring the contents of the pot to within 1 inch of the brim of the pot. Bring to a boil. Lower heat and simmer for 30 minutes. Stir once or twice to make sure the noodles and potatoes do not stick to the bottom. Serving size = 1 cup.

Mushroom and Broccoli Omelettes

8 eggs (makes four omelettes)
1 (8 oz.) package fresh mushrooms or 1 can mushroom stems and pieces, drained

1 head of broccoli, separate florets from stalk and chop (save the rest for soup)
1 cup shredded cheddar cheese
Cooking spray

Beat two eggs in large bowl. Heat skillet on medium heat and spray with cooking spray. Pour eggs into skillet and swirl to cover the bottom of the skillet. Sprinkle each omelette with 2 oz. of mushrooms, ¼ of the broccoli florets, ¼ cup of cheese, salt and pepper to taste. Cover and reduce pan heat to low. After about 2 minutes, fold the omelette in half using a spatula. Cook a few minutes more until cheese is melted and egg is set. Remove from pan. Either serve immediately or place in a serving dish in a 250° oven to hold until all omelettes are ready to serve. Repeat for each two-egg omelette.

Open-Faced Tuna Melts

2 (5 oz.) cans tuna
2 tablespoons Miracle Whip or mayonnaise
½ teaspoon onion powder
Dash of pepper

4 slices of cheddar cheese (or American cheese slices)
4 slices bread (any type you have on hand will work)

Combine tuna, Miracle Whip, onion powder, and pepper in a bowl. Turn on broiler. Place bread slices on cookie sheet. Put cookie sheet in oven on a rack next to the broiler. Broil bread until lightly toasted on one side. Remove from oven. Turn bread over. Divide tuna mixture between the four slices of bread and spread. Place one slice of cheese on top of tuna mixture for each sandwich. Return to oven. Broil until cheese is bubbly and slightly browned. Watch closely as they can burn quickly. Serves four.

Pink Salmon with Pineapple Brown Sugar Rice

1 (15 oz.) can of pink salmon
3 tablespoons Miracle Whip or mayonnaise
1 teaspoon onion powder
1 teaspoon dried parsley
A dash of paprika

2 cups rice (white or brown or mix 1 cup of each)
½ (15 oz.) can crushed pineapple
1 tablespoon brown sugar
4 cups water

Put rice, pineapple, brown sugar, and water into a rice cooker. Start the cooker. If you do not have a rice cooker, cook the rice mixture on the stove following the package directions. Meanwhile, mix pink salmon, Miracle Whip, onion powder and dried parsley in a bowl. Serve rice in a bowl with a ¼ cup (½ cup) of salmon mixture and sautéed vegetables on top. Sprinkle with paprika. Serves eight.

Sautéed Vegetables

½ cup chopped onion
1 cup each green beans, corn, peppers

2 tablespoons canola or olive oil

Heat oil in skillet over medium heat. Add onions, cook until translucent, about 5 minutes. Add other vegetables. Cook until vegetables are slightly browned. Stir with spatula occasionally during cooking. Serving size = ½ cup.

Tender Herbed Chicken

1 to 2 lbs chicken pieces (use thighs, drumsticks, tenderloins, breasts from the bags of frozen chicken pieces or cut up one whole chicken)
2/3 cup salad oil
2 tablespoons parsley, chopped

1 teaspoon salt (optional)
1 teaspoon seasoned salt
1 teaspoon Italian seasoning
½ teaspoon paprika
¼ teaspoon black pepper

Place chicken in a shallow pan. Mix remaining ingredients; pour over chicken and let stand 2 hours, turning occasionally. (You could also do this in a gallon-size zip-lock bag.) Drain off marinade and reserve. Brown chicken in a hot skillet. Place browned chicken in a shallow baking dish. Pour ½ cup reserved marinade in bottom of the pan. Cover with aluminum foil. Cook in 350° oven for about 60 minutes. Chicken is done when thick part of thigh or breast cuts easily with no pink showing. (It should be "fall off the bone" tender.) Serving size = 4 ounces.

Turkey Sausage Casserole

1 lb turkey sausage
½ of a 16 oz. package of elbow macaroni
1 (15 oz.) can of stewed tomatoes
2 teaspoon dried onion

1 teaspoon Italian spices (or ½ teaspoon oregano and ½ teaspoon basil)
1 teaspoon Worchestershire sauce
½ cup grated cheddar cheese

Pre-heat oven to 350°. Cook macaroni according to package directions. Drain. Brown turkey sausage in a skillet. Mix stewed tomatoes with dried onion, Italian spices, and Worchestershire sauce in a large bowl. Add noodles and cooked sausage to the sauce mix and stir. Pour mixture into a 13- X 9-inch baking dish. Sprinkle with cheddar cheese. Cover with foil. Bake for 45 minutes. Remove foil and bake ten more minutes or until cheese is bubbly and lightly browned. Makes 8 servings.

Appendix B: Substitutions

Instead of rushing to the store when you run out of something, use these easy substitutions. You will save money by using what you have on hand. Also, studies show each time a person visits a store more items are bought than originally intended. Save yourself the temptation to overspend.

Baking powder: 1 teaspoon baking powder = ½ teaspoon cream of tarter + ¼ teaspoon baking soda

Brown sugar: 1 cup brown sugar = 1 cup white sugar + 2 tablespoons molasses

Butter: ½ cup salted butter = ½ cup unsalted butter + ¼ teaspoon salt. If you have salted butter and the recipe calls for unsalted butter, omit ¼ teaspoon salt for each ½ cup butter.

Buttermilk: 1 cup buttermilk = 1 teaspoon lemon juice (or vinegar) and enough milk to make one cup.

Chocolate, semisweet: 1 ounce semisweet chocolate = 3 tablespoons semisweet chocolate chips or 1 ounce unsweetened chocolate + 1 tablespoon sugar

Chocolate, unsweetened: 1 ounce unsweetened chocolate = 3 tablespoons unsweetened cocoa powder + 1 tablespoon butter

Corn syrup, dark: 1 cup dark corn syrup = ¾ cup light corn syrup + ¼ cup molasses

Cornstarch: 1 tablespoon corn starch = 2 tablespoons flour

Flour, cake: 1 cup cake flour = ¾ cup + 2 tablespoons flour + 2 tablespoons corn starch, sifted together

Flour, self-rising: 2 cups self-rising flour = 2 cups flour + 1 teaspoon baking soda + 2 teaspoons baking powder + 1 teaspoon salt

Garlic: 1 clove fresh garlic = 1/8 teaspoon garlic powder

Garlic salt: 1 teaspoon garlic salt = 1/8 teaspoon garlic powder + enough salt to make 1 teaspoon

Ginger: 1 teaspoon fresh ginger = ¼ teaspoon powdered ginger

Half-and-half: 1 cup half-and-half = 1 tablespoon melted butter and enough whole milk to make 1 cup

Herbs: 1 tablespoon fresh herbs = 1 teaspoon dried herbs

Lemon juice: 1 teaspoon lemon juice = ¼ teaspoon cider vinegar
(1 medium lemon will give 2 to 3 tablespoons of juice.)

Lime: 1 medium lime = 1 ½ to 2 tablespoons of juice

Milk: 1 cup whole milk = ½ cup evaporated milk + ½ cup water

Mustard, prepared: =½ teaspoon ground mustard mixed with 2 teaspoons vinegar

Onion: 1 small, chopped onion = 1 teaspoon onion powder or 1 tablespoon dried minced onion

Pumpkin pie spice: 1 teaspoon pumpkin pie spice = ¼ teaspoon nutmeg + ¼ teaspoon ginger + ½ teaspoon cinnamon

Sour Cream: 1 cup sour cream = 1 cup plain yogurt

Sugar: 1 cup sugar = 2 cups powdered sugar (Do not substitute in baking!)

Tapioca: 2 teaspoons tapioca = 1 tablespoon flour

Yeast, active dry: 1 envelope = 2 ¼ to 2 ½ teaspoons of yeast

Appendix C: Conversions

Dry:
3 teaspoons = 1 tablespoon
16 tablespoons = 1 cup
12 tablespoons = ¾ cup
10 tablespoons + 2 teaspoons = ²/₃ cup
8 tablespoons = ½ cup
6 tablespoons = ³/₈ cup
5 tablespoons + 1 teaspoon = ¹/₃ cup
4 tablespoons = ¼ cup
2 tablespoons = ¹/₈ cup

Liquid:
2 cups = 1 pint
2 pints = 1 quart
4 quarts = 1 gallon
16 ounces = 1 pint
32 ounces = 1 quart
64 ounces = 2 quarts = ½ gallon
128 ounces = 1 gallon

Dry to Cooked Equivalents:
Beans, dried: 1 lb (2 ½ cups) = 6 cups cooked
Macaroni, elbow: 8 ounces (2 cups) = 4 cups cooked
Noodles: 8 ounces (4 cups) = 4 to 4 ½ cups cooked
Peas, dried: 1 pound (2 cups) = 5 cups cooked
Rice, regular: 1 cup dried = 3 cups cooked
Rice, instant: 1 cup dried = 2 cups cooked
Spaghetti: 8 ounces = 4 cups cooked

Dry:
8 ounces = 1 cup
16 ounces = 2 cups

Appendix D: Reading a Food Label

Look for products which contain mostly polyunsaturated and monosaturated fats rather than saturated fats.

Recommended daily intake of cholesterol is less than 200mg.

Dietary Fiber should total between 25 to 38 grams per day.

United States Department of Agriculture advises adults who eat a 2,000-calorie diet to limit consumption of sugar to about 40 grams (10 teaspoons) of added sugars per day.

Look for hydrogenated oils and artificial sweeteners in the ingredients section. Hydrogenated oils which produce less than 0g will not show up in the Trans Fat listing higher up on the label but may still be in the product. Only buy products which do not use hydrogenated oils. Artificial sweeteners have been linked to diseases like depression. You may wish to avoid these products.

Nutrition Facts

Serving Size 15 crackers (30g)
Servings Per Container About 8

Amount Per Serving

Calories 150   Calories from Fat 60

% Daily Value*

Total Fat 7g	11%
Saturated Fat 1.5g	8%
Trans Fat 0g	
Polyunsaturated Fat 3.5g	
Monounsaturated Fat 1.5g	
Cholesterol 0mg	0%
Sodium 230mg	10%
Potassium 35mg	1%
Total Carbohydrate 18g	6%
Dietary Fiber <1g	3%
Sugars 3g	
Protein 2g	

Vitamin A 6%		Vitamin C 2%
Calcium 6%		Iron 6%
Folic Acid 0%		

*Percent Daily Values are based on a 2,000 calorie diet. Your daily values may be higher or lower depending on your calorie needs:

		Calories	2,000	2,500
Total Fat	Less Than		65g	80g
Saturated Fat	Less Than		20g	25g
Cholesterol	Less Than		300mg	300mg
Sodium	Less Than		2,400mg	2,400mg
Potassium			3,500mg	3,500mg
Total Carbohydrate			300g	375g
Dietary Fiber			25g	30g

Calories per gram
Fat 9 • Carbohydrate 4 • Protein 4

INGREDIENTS: ENRICHED FLOUR (WHEAT FLOUR, NIACIN, REDUCED IRON, THIAMIN MONONITRATE [VITAMIN B1], RIBOFLAVIN [VITAMIN B2], FOLIC ACID), CANOLA OIL AND/OR PALM OIL AND/OR SOYBEAN OIL WITH TBHQ FOR FRESHNESS, SUGAR, SALSA AND CREAM CHEESE SEASONING (GARLIC POWDER, CITRIC ACID, MALTODEXTRIN, CULTURED NONFAT MILK, MODIFIED FOOD STARCH, NATURAL FLAVORS, DEHYDRATED PARSLEY, DEHYDRATED BELL PEPPER, EXTRACTIVE OF PAPRIKA, CORN SYRUP SOLIDS, SODIUM CASEINATE, VINEGAR, ARTIFICIAL FLAVOR, SILICON DIOXIDE [TO PREVENT CAKING], SOYBEAN OIL), MODIFIED FOOD STARCH, WHEAT GLUTEN, CONTAINS TWO PERCENT OR LESS OF: HIGH FRUCTOSE CORN SYRUP, LEAVENING (BAKING SODA, CALCIUM PHOSPHATE), SALT, SOY LECITHIN (EMULSIFIER), SODIUM SULFITE.
ALLERGY WARNING: CONTAINS MILK, WHEAT AND SOY.

Use the serving size to give the correct amount for each meal.

Look for products that have no Trans Fats which have been found to harm your health.

Sodium levels should be low. The 2010 Dietary Guidelines for Americans recommend limiting sodium to less than 2,300 mg a day — or 1,500 mg if you're age 51 or older, or if you are black, or if you have high blood pressure, diabetes or chronic kidney disease.

Recommended daily amount of protein for children ages 1-8 is 13-19g; for children ages 9-13 is 34g; for women is 46g; and for men 56g.

If someone in the family has food allergies, the allergy warning is very important. A product may not only contain food allergens, but could have been made in a factory which processes food containing an allergen.

www.ingramcontent.com/pod-product-compliance
Lightning Source LLC
Chambersburg PA
CBHW081639040426
42449CB00014B/3381